This book belongs to

_____

Feelings Ninja

By Mary Nhin

Pictures by
Jelena Stupar

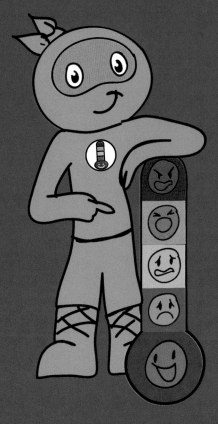

This book is dedicated to my children - Mikey, Kobe, and Jojo.

Ninja Life Hacks™

I jumped out of bed, pulled back the curtains, and stretched on my tippy toes.

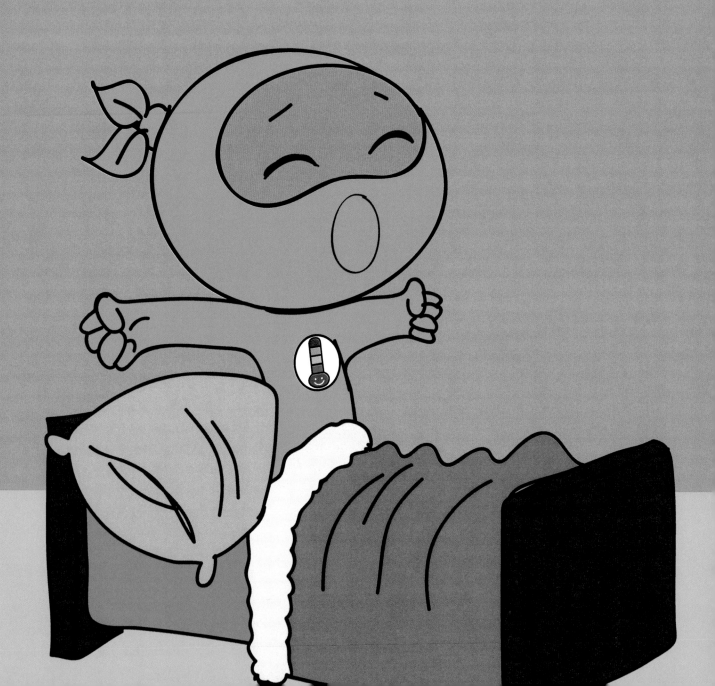

It was going to be a beautiful day. I was just sure of it.

After breakfast, I went outside to catch some hoops. But when I grabbed my basketball, I became disappointed to learn that it wouldn't bounce.

Then, the doorbell rang. It was Frustrated Ninja.

I was so happy to see my friend!

I like using a Feelings Thermometer to check the temperature of my feelings. This helps me to recognize the feeling that I'm experiencing so I can choose the best reaction.

Feelings Thermometer:

How do you feel?	What can you do about it?
ANGRY, FURIOUS, EXPLOSIVE >Yelling, Stomping, Meltdown	Physical exercise, Deep breathing, Count to ten
FRUSTRATED, ANNOYED, IRRITABLE >Arguing, Shutting down	Meditate, Listen to music, Exercise, Ask for help
ANXIOUS, WORRIED, UNSETTLED >Pacing, Avoiding, Clingy	Talk to someone, Focus on what you can control, Practice grounding by using your five senses
SAD, NEGATIVE, LONELY >Crying, Withdrawn, Disengaged	Use positive self talk, Talk to a friend, Journal about your feelings
POSITIVE, CALM, HAPPY >Smiling, Laughing, Engaged	Help someone else, Do something fun, Notice and enjoy your mood

If you listen to what your body tells you, it gives you clues so you know what you're feeling...

POSITIVE

Mouth is smiling

Voice is enthusiastic

Muscles tighten

Clenched fists and teeth

Face is happy

FURIOUS

Shoulders hunch

I had never thought about it like that! That evening, I drew a Feelings Thermometer in my journal and made a chart. I posted it on my wall.

How do you feel? / What can you do about it?

How do you feel?	What can you do about it?
ANGRY, FURIOUS, EXPLOSIVE >Yelling, Stomping, Meltdown	Physical exercise, Deep breathing, Count to ten
FRUSTRATED, ANNOYED, IRRITABLE >Arguing, Shutting down	Meditate, Listen to music, Exercise, Ask for help
ANXIOUS, WORRIED, UNSETTLED >Pacing, Avoiding, Clingy	Talk to someone, Focus on what you can control, Practice grounding by using your five senses
SAD, NEGATIVE, LONELY >Crying, Withdrawn, Disengaged	Use positive self talk, Talk to a friend, Journal about your feelings
 POSITIVE, CALM, HAPPY >Smiling, Laughing, Engaged	Help someone else, Do something fun, Notice and enjoy your mood

Kinda cool.

The next day, I experienced a range of emotions. But it was different this time. I could tell what I was feeling and respond to it in a more proactive way by using my Feelings Thermometer.

For example, when I went to go brush my teeth, I tripped over a toy my sister had left on the floor. I got so angry and wanted to scream. But then, I thought about checking my temperature on the Feelings Thermometer.

You're angry. Let's take a deep breath and calmly ask her to pick up her things.

When I went into the kitchen, I found out my mom had made my favorite breakfast. I was so happy. I recognized what a positive mood I was in. I thanked my mom and asked her if she needed any help.

It wasn't long until my feelings changed again. In the middle of building a structure, I became upset that the directions didn't make sense. I thought to myself, *Time to check my temperature.* I, then, realized I was feeling frustrated.

Okay, what do I do with frustration? Ahhh yes, I can ask for help, I thought.

Having a Feelings Thermometer really helped me recognize and manage my feelings!

I feel very grateful to Frustrated Ninja for introducing me to this cool tool!

Download your Feelings Thermometer, Feelings Weather Forecast, and beyond the book resources at ninjalifehacks.tv

Made in the USA
Las Vegas, NV
15 October 2021